W. B Mitchell

Dollars, or, What?

A Little Common Sense Applied to Silver as Money

W. B Mitchell

Dollars, or, What?
A Little Common Sense Applied to Silver as Money

ISBN/EAN: 9783744720038

Printed in Europe, USA, Canada, Australia, Japan

Cover: Foto ©ninafisch / pixelio.de

More available books at **www.hansebooks.com**

DOLLARS,

OR, WHAT?

A Little Common Sense

Applied to Silver as Money.

By W. B. MITCHELL.

TIMES PRINT, CHATTANOOGA, TENN.

The articles in the following pages are, many of them,
particularly suitable on account of brevity, for newspaper
clipping and quotation. It was the writer's purpose to
make them acceptable to the general reader by reason of
simplicity of statement as well as brevity. He trusts that
enough merit may be found in them to induce liberal quotations, which all journals are at liberty to make, if credit
is given for same, it being through this source partly that
he has hoped to reach the masses with the sound doctrines
he endeavors to teach. And

To the Newspapers of the Land

THIS LITTLE WORK IS

... Dedicated ...

PREFACE.

IT has occurred to the author of the following pages that nearly all writers on financial questions assume that readers generally understand the salient principles of finance and banking, and they therefore fail to reach the understanding of the masses. And though these principles are few, and not mysterious, many of our most intelligent and capable men, particularly in professional life, have given scant attention to such matters; and many men of abundant sense in agricultural and other pursuits have had little opportunity to study them. With the view of appealing to these good citizens, who are always desirous of forming correct opinions on important public issues, but who have not the time nor possibly the patience to carefully wade through conflicting newspaper comments and reports, the author has written a number of short articles on the most important question that has come before the American people since the days of slavery. He has not gone extensively into statistics, nor into a scientific discussion of the subjects he handles, but has merely grouped a few simple facts and principles and presented them in a plain, direct manner; such as will, he trusts, make them understood by all who may read them. He appeals directly to the common sense of the people. He does not believe the financial question a complicated or a difficult one, as it is generally supposed to be; but on the contrary, quite understandable and easy of solution if the people were agreed on the main issue; and he attempts in plain language to make it as plain to others as it appears to him.

Although a banker, where he owns one dollar in bank stock he owns ten dollars in other property. He believes that a bank cannot prosper unless the customers and the community prosper, and that the prosperity of these depends upon the prosperity of the country as a whole; but if it were possible that the prosperity of the bank he manages lay in one direction and the prosperity of the people and the country lay in another direction, his self-interest would oblige and compel him to go with the people and the country. He therefore speaks, not as a banker, but as an American citizen. He speaks, also, as a Southern man, concerned for the future of the South. He believes that the South has a great future under right conditions. He believes that the agitation of free silver is a blight upon the South, and that its industries and enterprises must, in a measure, await the settlement of the free coinage issue.

The chief and only serious plea the free silver advocates make for the favor of voters is that "demonetization" of silver has been the cause of the steady decline in most values since 1873, and that its free coinage would restore values and advance silver to the prices of former years. Particular care is taken in the following pages to show the error of this view.

An effort is also made to show the danger of inflation in any form, and that stability and confidence are the basis of all prosperity.

Statistics given are taken from the 1894 United States government reports, unless otherwise specified, approximate figures being generally used.

Certain repetition is used in some intances, with the view of making each article more forcible and a more complete argument within itself, the writer believing that short articles are more likely to be read and understood than any long and continuous exposition of the questions involved. The writer appeals with earnest purpose to the voter, and begs a careful, thoughtful reading of what he says. We all live in the same country, and our interests in this matter are the same. If calamity befalls us, none can dodge its shadow; if prosperity smiles upon us, all alike are filled with gladness.

W. B. MITCHELL.

Chattanooga, Tenn., April 16th, 1895.

CONTENTS.

DOLLARS, OR WHAT?

VOTERS RIGHT MINDED.

It is a mistake to charge that all the free silver people are fanatics, lunatics and repudiationists. A mistake as great as it is to say that sound money men are "conspirators" and "gold bugs." Many of them are among our most useful and intelligent citizens, and are perfectly honest and patriotic. They have not seriously studied the merits of the doctrines they embrace, but they are as anxious as any of us to do the right thing and put the country in the way of prosperity. They are open to argument and to conviction. They somehow have an idea that there is a "conspiracy" to drive out silver and to "contract" the currency. The metal has been "demonetized," and that to them is an ominous and misleading word. They do not know that much more silver has been coined and circulated since the alleged "demonetization" than before, and that we have fully seven times as much now as in 1873. They do not understand that free silver means the driving out of gold, and leaving silver and paper only as money. They do not understand that such calamity would suddenly contract the currency more than if all the silver in the country were dumped into the sea. Their feelings and their sentiments have been played upon by demagogues, and it is these men who deserve the severest condemnation. Most of these have had opportunities of information, and know the falsity of their statements. But their business is politics. They are after fat berths in government service. They are, or want to be Congressmen and Senators, at salaries they could not earn at home, even if they were willing to work. They deceive and misrepresent for a selfish purpose. It pays them in dollars and cents to do it. Some of them are high in party and national councils, and the people, respecting high station, have learned to respect them and to be guided by them. What is here said does not apply to all free silver politicians, nor to all politicians of any party or faction, but, as must be owned, it applies truthfully to the great majority of them. And the free silver advocates are now making more false statements, and doing more mischief than any other class of office seekers. And there is but one way to checkmate them. That is to give the people the facts in such way that they may be understood. When this is well done the day of the free coinage trickster is done.

The road to financial ruin will not be followed when the sign-boards are well posted. Sensible men—and most voters are sensible—do not rush into pitfalls when the marks are clear. These can, and should be made clear as day.

THE FINANCIAL QUESTION.

The money question is now the most vital issue in American politics, and it is one on which the demagogue can get in his most effective work. He needs no experience, practical ability, nor brains, to belabor the "gold bugs," and the "money power," and to talk about the "dollar of our daddies," and the "money of the constitution."

Whether he be a brilliant but deluded theorist, a shrewd and designing owner of Western silver mines, or a cheap politician who takes the shortest cut to get votes, he is a dangerous agitator, because he appeals to popular, though mistaken, prejudices.

A combination of adverse causes and conditions depressed values and trade throughout the world, and the fear of a silver basis has intensified that depression in America. The free silver advocate, if he be a misguided theorist, believes, and if he be a silver mine owner or a mere demagogue, pretends to believe, that these conditions are the direct result of what he calls "demonetization" of silver. He attributes all legislation "unfriendly" to silver, the world over, to the "gold bugs," thus appealing to the prejudice of those who do not think and reason for themselves. His false doctrines are the more readily accepted because the government itself, first from supposed necessity during the rebellion, and since under the direction of unwise and compromising politicians, has upheld the vicious theory of fiat money and inflation. It first became a bank of issue, and undertook to furnish the people with fiat paper money, and then for purposes of individual gain it was saddled with the product of the Western silver mines, and soon began.to issue fiat silver, continuing this dangerous experiment till the world began to doubt its solvency, and gave its strange system and money the cold shoulder. Foreign investors began to withdraw from the country, and the panic of 1893 was the result. The Sherman law was repealed, and the issue of fiat money was stopped. But the weakness and folly of our financial system had been laid bare, and recovery was slow. Our slender gold reserve, which supported our great volume of fiat money, and our thousands of millions of credits of all kinds, was in evident danger. The danger was intensified when the Fifty-Third Congress—an incompetent, free silver body—assembled. And during the existence of that Congress the country was kept in a state of feverish anxiety and uncertainty.

It is a matter of great concern to us all that we get back to a safe and sensible financial policy. Whether we toil at the desk or in the workshop, behind the counter or on the farm, we are each and all directly concerned in having a stable financial system, in the permanency and safety of which we, and outsiders, have absolute faith.

We want to be paid for our labor in good money, which we can put by with confidence. If we buy anything with it we want the full worth of good money; if we put it at interest, put it in the bank, or invest it in securities or life insurance, we do not want it returned to us or to our families at a discount. We want to make safe, and not speculative investments with our savings. We earn good dollars, and we do not want to see them depreciate and become bad dollars, whether in our own or in other hands. We lock up a hundred cents, or we put out a hundred cents, and we want it to remain a hundred cents. We do not want it to shrink to seventy-five cents or to fifty cents while we are about our work or our business. We do not want to go to bed at night with a dollar and get up in the morning with less than a dollar. We do not want an uncertain or a fluctuating currency. If we are wise we want the standard of all great civilized nations.

We have good investments to offer. We have a new country with great natural resources. We want the confidence of people all over the world—want their brains and enterprise and money to aid in developing these resources. We have now, in a measure, lost that confidence, and can obtain it again only by manifesting the clearest purpose of future integrity in our national finances. If we lend an ear to the delusive harangues of the free silver advocate, it is hopelessly gone from us.

We of the South in particular are vitally concerned in a financial policy that will insure the confidence of everybody. We have the richest undeveloped section of the country. The eyes of investors everywhere are turned toward us. Give the country safe financial legislation and within ten years the idle accumulation of money of the East and of other countries would come to us by the hundreds of millions. But give us free coinage of silver and we shall invite the ridicule and contempt of the civilized world. We should take a backward step of half a century in our industrial growth. Under such condition there would be no hope at all for the present generation in the South. The East, with its generations of savings and large accumulations, might, in a way, survive such a calamity, largely, too, at our cost; but we should flounder in poverty.

Without regard to political ties or associations, let us of the South, aye, and of the North, and the East, rise and stand together against this proposed and monstrous blunder. Let us make it clear that no man, of any party, can have our votes unless he squarely defines himself for honest money and honest financial legislation.

DIVISIONS OF SENTIMENT.

Bimetallism means the use of both gold and silver as money. It does not necessarily mean a double standard, which is an impossibility, unless an equal intrinsic marketable value of metal is put in each kind of dollar. That is, 100 cents' worth of marketable gold in the gold dollar and 100 cents' worth of marketable silver in the silver dollar. This would make a double standard, but to remain so there must be no fluctuation in the market value of either metal.

The use of gold alone as a money metal is gold monometallism.

The use of silver alone is silver monometallism.

The silver mining states of the West want and have long been striving for silver monometallism.

The remainder of the free silver people want bimetallism.

The distinction is vital, but not generally understood, or recognized.

There is really wider difference of real sentiment between the mining camps of the West and the silver people of other sections than there is between the latter and the sound money men.

Silver men east of the Mississippi have no interest in the silver product as an industry, and only desire to promote its wider use as money; but generally, unlike their Western allies, they would oppose its use to the exclusion of gold and the great consequent reduction in the volume of our currency.

They have a mistaken theory that gold and silver can both become standards of money on a basis of 16 to 1, and it is that theory for which they are earnestly fighting, in the honest but erroneous belief that it would work in practice and restore old time prosperity. It is simply a theory, because it is an idea or scheme that has never been put to the test. There is no record in history that any nation has attempted to make standards of two metals at a ratio of greatly different values.

The silver people assert that free coinage would raise the value of silver to that of gold on a basis of 16 to 1, but that is also a mere theory, with everything against it and nothing in favor of it, excepting the bare assertion, and that, like the other, is a most dangerous theory in view of the calamities its test would precipitate.

The sound money men oppose both these theories, and also oppose the scheme of the Western silverites to put the country on a silver basis, with silver as the only metallic currency. They are not gold monometallists, as is often charged. There is no public sentiment favoring gold monometallism in this country. They are bimetallists, differing from the free coinage bimetallists in that they favor our present gold standard of value, and desire to keep all the silver that can be safely used, and all the paper circulation as good as gold, on which both are based.

Unlike the free coinage bimetallists, they advocate no theories. They adhere to precedents and tried principles.

They believe that the experiences and practical financial tests of other nations, at the present day and in former periods, are a safe guide. They have the record of a thousand years of financiering, and find no instance where a bold and generally distrusted financial theory, put to a practical test, has not wrought disaster. Although they greatly admire the genius of young America, and are partial to some of her statesmen, they are unwilling to follow the lead of men who would make such radical departure from all known and tried methods of financiering.

The writer believes this to be a true and candid statement of three important divisions of sentiment on the financial question.

Is the reader a bimetallist of the theoretical school? Is he a bimetallist of the practical school? Or is he a silver monometallist of the school of the mining camps?

If he is a bimetallist of the theoretical school, there is great hope that he may join the practical school. It is assumed that he is a sensible, right thinking man, earnest in right purposes, really afraid of mere theories; and if he will take the pains to investigate this important matter he can ascertain that his present views ARE theoretical to the extent that they have never been tried by ANY nation that history makes mention of.

If, however, he belongs to the school of the mining camps, there is little hope of him. They have silver to sell out there, and the only lessons taught are how to sell it. This is a selfish doctrine, and the man who embraces it is hard to reach. There are a few politicians east of the Mississippi who belong to this school, but they have outlived their day and usefulness.

THE GOVERNMENT STAMP ON MONEY.

It is a popular error of free coinage people, and other advocates of fiat money, that the stamp of the government makes money perfectly good. This false idea is at the bottom of most inflation theories.

The United States, or any other government, might stamp a dollar mark on a paper bill and it would not pass for 5 cents, nor for 1 cent, if the bill were drawn without any promise to pay. This is a simple fact, not at all understood by many intelligent people.

There must be a promise of final redemption, acceptance for customs, or other substantial promise to pay, and its value, as money, depends entirely on the kind of payment promised, and on the solvency and ability of the government or institution issuing the bill. In Mexico, or any other country on a silver basis, the promise to pay would be in silver, and the bill, therefore, granting the solvency and promptness of the maker, would be worth a Mexican silver dollar, about fifty cents of our money.

In the United States the promise to pay on such bill means payment in gold, because the United States maintains a supply of gold for the special purpose of paying any of these bills that may be presented.

Another mistaken idea of many uninformed people is that the government issues these bills, and that they pass from hand to hand indefinitely, and nobody ever asks to have them redeemed.

The fact is that the government is often called on for the redemption of its bills. This has been made quite clear and become pretty generally understood during the past two years. Business men require gold for commercial purposes, and when it suits their convenience they exchange their paper money for it. But if such exchange seldom, or never, actually occurred, the fact that it could at any time be made would make the paper money as good as gold.

A man may have $100 to his credit in bank, and let it remain there year after year, because he does not need it, and believes if he should need it he could go to the bank and get it.

Under our system the government represents the bank, and the holder of any bill, or piece of money other than gold, represents the depositor, and the bill or money he holds is a certificate of deposit. As long as he can go to the government bank and get this certificate cashed, he is satisfied to hold it; or the man he owes, or deals with, willingly accepts it. In other words, if the government clearly shows its purpose of maintaining, and its ability to maintain, its gold reserve for redemption purposes, no large volume of paper, or fiat money, is presented for redemption. But if the government wavers in that purpose, or if it puts in circulation too many promises to pay, either in paper dollars or in silver dollars—if it thus increases its demand obligations out of proportion to the gold redemption reserve, then people lose confidence in the intrinsic value of its dollar marks on paper and silver, and large amounts of the money are taken to the treasury and exchanged for gold, as was the case after the passage of the Sherman law, and notably in 1893.

During the ten years preceding the passage of the Sherman act the total withdrawals of gold from the treasury, in exchange for paper money, were less than twenty millions of dollars; but during the four years the Sherman law was in force these withdrawals of gold exceeded two hundred and sixty millions of dollars. Had that law not been repealed in 1893, there would not have been a.dollar of gold in the treasury within six months, and there would soon have been none in the country. We should have wholly lost more than one-third of the money in circulation, and the remaining two-thirds would have been on a silver basis, possessing only one-half its former purchasing value.

The United States has no more immunity from distrust, if it manages its finances badly, than an individual or a corporate institution. If conducted on unsound principles, its treasury is as liable to a run as a bank.· If people have paper bills with dollar marks on them, for which they can get gold today but may not be able to get it tomorrow, they are apt to make the exchange today. If they have silver pieces worth really only 50 cents, but which, by reason of the government stamp, and promise, they can now convert into gold, but may not be able .to do so to-morrow or next week, they are likely to convert it now. And it is not bankers only who make the exchange.

There are to-day tens of millions of gold hoarded in the stockings of the free silver coinage advocates of the United States. The writer knows a man in his own city, prominent in public life and a pronounced free coinage man, who in 1893 promptly converted his bank account into gold and locked it up. He knows scores of other strong free silver men who did the same thing.

In practice these people appear to know the difference between a dollar mark and a real dollar—between a gold basis and a silver basis; but in theory the "money of the constitution" is good enough for anybody, and a gold standard is infamous.

DIFFERENCE BETWEEN DEMAND AND TIME OBLIGATIONS.

Persons who do not reason, and have given small attention to business principles and financial matters, do not recognize the difference between demand and time obligations, particularly as applied to governmental affairs.

They know that the United States is a great and rich country, and that it is abundantly able to pay all its debts. They reason that such a great country, with such unlimited resources, can put out unlimited quantities of paper, or depreciated silver, and circulate them at full face value as money. But, as stated elsewhere, such money must be promises to pay; and to make the promise good the government must be ready to pay. It must be ready to pay on demand. If not, the promise means nothing. Its promise to pay must be in something of intrinsic value. Gold, if on a gold basis, and silver if on a silver basis, and this redemption money must be in hand and in sight. It must be in good proportion to the money it puts in circulation. If it is not, nobody has confidence in the money. But the ability of any government to accumulate and carry a stock of coin for such purpose is limited, and consequently its circulation of money must be limited in proportion.

Time obligations are less directly limited. These are based on the resources and wealth of the country; on its revenue, or possible revenue. They may be paid at maturity, or funded and extended indefinitely. They bear interest, and can be floated as long as there is no decline in the resources of the country.

Demand obligations, in the form of money, bear no interest, and are therefore of uncertain value, whether issued by a government or by an authorized corporation, unless good on demand.

The United States can float its 10, 20 or 30-year interest-bearing bonds in very large sums, without injury to its credit, but floating money, payable on demand, and

on which payment is being constantly demanded, is quite
a different thing.

The distinction is vital. There would be less clamor
for fiat money if it were generally better understood.

An individual with good resources may put out $10,000
of his interest-bearing time notes and carry such indebtedness for years.

Before they mature he prudently arranges for renewals,
or places them elsewhere. If these obligations were payable on demand they would be a constant menace, liable
to bankrupt him at any time.

Fundamental principles of business and finance are
inexorable, and apply relentlessly alike to men or nations.

Any scheme to issue large amounts of fiat money is
wholly chimerical. Wherever undertaken the result has
been failure and bankruptcy. No people can grow rich
on promises to pay that cannot be made good.

A DOUBLE MONETARY STANDARD.

The only way a double standard of money can be maintained is to put the same commercial value of metal in the
coin of each standard. If an actual dollar's worth of silver be put in the silver dollar, and a dollar's worth of gold
in the gold dollar, then the gold dollar and the silver dollar will both become standards. Commercial laws will
make them such without any reference to legislation.
Commercial law is superior to legislation in the fixing of
values.

It is a wholly mistaken and visionary theory that legislation (either by one government or by all the govern-
ments in the world) can make a double standard of money,
or of anything else. Is it reasonable to suppose that the
United States and all Europe combined could pass laws
that would make the prices of wheat and corn the same
in the world's markets? And yet the prices of these commodities can as easily be regulated as the values of gold
and silver. If 50 cents or 75 cents, or even 99 cents' worth
of silver be put into the silver dollar, and both the gold
dollar and the silver dollar are made a legal tender
(without a gold redemption feature), it ought to be easy
enough to see that people would use the cheaper dollar,

and either sell or hoard the dollar of greater intrinsic value. The silver dollar would be as good as the gold dollar to pay debts with, but the gold dollar would sell in the market by weight for a premium. Therefore, the gold would go out of circulation. It is simply impossible to keep two moneys of different intrinsic values both in circulation, unless the cheaper money is made redeemable in the more valuable money.

And an unlimited amount of cheap money cannot be redeemable in good money.

Up to twenty years ago the ratio of value between the two metals had been for about two centuries between 14 1-2 and 16 of silver to 1 of gold. Running thus evenly it was not impossible to have a double money standard, and such standard did exist in many countries.

But at times one metal or the other increased or decreased in value, and at such times the more valuable in every instance went out of circulation.

This is the record of history, and many instances may be cited. It is only within comparatively recent years that any country conceived the plan of making the cheaper metal redeemable in or interchangeable with the more valuable metal. And when silver began to be so abundant, and to decline so greatly, all countries, excepting the United States, abandoned or greatly modified that plan.

INCONSISTENCY OF FREE COINAGE ADVOCATES.

The worst inconsistency of the advocate of free coinage is the ratio at which he insists silver must be coined. He wants it coined at 16 to 1. That is, he would put 16 times as much weight in a silver dollar as is put in a gold dollar. On this basis, before either piece of metal is converted into stamped money, the piece of gold would sell in any market in the world for 100 cents, whereas the piece of silver would bring but little over 50 cents.

It is clear that the silver 50-cent piece must be made by law interchangeable with and practically redeemable by the government in the full value gold dollar; otherwise the two dollars would not circulate side by side. Yet this silver theorist rails at the government for keeping a gold reserve to make this 50-cent silver money pass for 100 cents.

If silver advocates want to coin all the silver in the world why do they not propose to put 100 cents' worth of silver into the silver dollar? It would then stand alone, and until silver declined they could, without disturbance, give the metal the "wide use" to which they claim it is entitled.

The writer does not believe in nor advocate the practicability of this policy, but speaks from the silver standpoint. And such policy would be more honest, and somewhat less dangerous than the plan proposed, though it would doubtless soon result in the disasters of the Sherman law.

In former ages and periods silver was in great request as a money medium, because the supply was very limited. But modern discoveries, appliances and inventions have so increased and cheapened the product that it is fast ceasing to be of value as a money metal. While in former ages it was turned out by the pound, it is now turned out by the ton and by the ship load. At one period of the world copper was used as money, and would doubtless have continued in use to the present day but for the fact that it became so abundant that it ceased to be a precious metal.

It is not easy for people now to accept the idea that silver may for the same reason eventually cease to be useful for monetary purposes. That time has not yet, and may never come, but it cannot be said to be a remote possibility.

It is foolish to go on theorizing about the cause of its decline, and the methods that would raise its value, when it is becoming so abundant that warehouses, instead of strong boxes, must be provided for its storage. The commercial law of supply and demand regulates its price exactly as it regulates the price of every other known product, and it is not within the power of all the legislative bodies in the world to permanently and materially raise or depress its value. Whether they all "demonetize" or "remonetize" makes in the long run small difference. The law of supply and demand has small respect for the edicts of legislative solons.

Happily, however, for other nations, and for the general good of mankind, the United States is the only coun-

try on earth dominated by the mine operators of a few
sparsely settled states.   England, France and Germany
may have a few visionaries, but their legislative bodies
are not bullied by a powerful lobby of millionaires with
train loads of silver for sale.

All efforts looking to free coinage bimetallism by inter-
national agreement are wasted.   The credits of Europe,
amounting to thousands of millions of dollars, are based
on a safe and permanent standard.   Its disturbance would
result in disaster and calamity, such as would shake to
the foundations every throne and government on the con-
tinent.   No step will be taken in the direction of such
danger.   And it is probable that even some of our free
silver mine owning Senators are not quite so blind as to
be unable to see the folly of expecting any move abroad
in that direction.   But they will clamor all the more for
renewed and enlarged "recognition" at home, on a basis
of 16 to 1, for their beloved metal.

VOLUME OF MONEY NEEDED.

Owing to the great number of banks, and the system
of credits throughout the United States, we need less
actual money per capita than is needed anywhere else in
the world.   There are few towns of five hundred population that have not a bank.   Less than 5 per cent. of all
payments are made in actual money.   The bank check
does the remainder.   A gives his check to B; the bank
transfers A's credit to B's account, and B checks in favor
of C, and so on through the alphabet.   This system of
ready credits does the work of a great volume of money.
It is not merely a convenience, but it increases profits in
prompt conversion and quick settlements.

Our money per capita of about $24 is, under our bank-
ing system, equal to a per capita of $100 in many coun-
tries.   We can make quicker turns and do more business
on $1 actual money than can be done on $5 in a country
that has few banks.

The banking capital of the United States exceeds one-
third of that of all the countries of Europe.   It amounts
to $1,400,000,000, against $3,500,000,000 in Europe.

The proportion of bank deposits in favor of this country is much greater. These are, in round figures: The United States, $4,000,000,000; Europe, $6,500,000,000.

It may be seen that we have about $60 per capita in deposits subject to call; and an immense volume of checks are in constant circulation. The total clearing house exchanges of the United States in 1894 amounted to $45,-615,000,000.* This is an incredible sum, and these exchanges supply the place of a great volume of money. Considering the aid of this circulation, we have much more money per capita than any other country. France, with $36 actual money per capita, has only about $20 per capita in bank deposits.

Another advantage we have is in the great number of small banks, widely scattered, and a corresponding number of small deposits, a large per cent. of which are, in the form of the bank check, constantly on the wing; and one must be a banker to know how much money people get the use of by sending checks all over the country before deposits are made to cover them. Many business firms constantly keep out thousands of dollars of checks with never a dollar of their own money in bank. They send these checks from Maine to California, making careful estimates as to how long it takes them to get round to the banks they are drawn on, and deposit money, or similar checks (the greater per cent. of deposits being other checks), in time to make them good. The volume of such checks, drawn against blank bank balances, is immense, and this class of checks alone answers for a large circulating medium.

We have an abundance of money in this country, if it were more evenly distributed as to sections. It unduly accumulates in the centers under our present currency system, and will continue to do so as long as the bulk of the money is issued directly by the government.

The great need of the South and other sections remote from the centers, is a flexible bank note currency. Not an issue by banks of the wildcat order, but a currency as good as the national bank note, though more flexible than that now is, and adapted to the varying seasons and conditions. The South has no interest in the Western silver mines. It has nothing to gain by unloading the product on the government. And it should turn its atten-

---

*Monetary Systems of the World.—Muhleman.

tion to its own practical needs, the most important of
which is a safe bank note currency. And particularly
so since a part of that plan would take the government
out of the banking business, relieve the treasury of its
disturbing embarrasments, and so hasten good times that
the Western miners would become a hopeless and a help-
less minority.*

ISSUING PAPER AGAINST SILVER.

One of the theories of the free silver advocate is that
the government can buy silver at about 60 cents an ounce,
and issue paper money—(generally called silver certificates)—against it on a basis of 16 to 1 of gold; which
would make $1 of the silver certificate represent less than
60 cents worth of silver held against it for its redemption.
In other words, if the government should buy say $55
worth of silver, it would be required to issue and put into
circulation $100 in silver certificates. (The exact cost of
the silver would depend on the market price at the time
of purchase.) The $55 worth of silver would be coined
into one hundred silver dollars, and any holder of the
certificates would be entitled to exchange them for the
coined silver. This was in part the principle of the Sherman law.

But as the writer has elsewhere clearly shown the mere
stamp of the government on paper gives it no value, unless there be a promise to pay, and to make the promise
trusted, it must be a promise of full payment.

Now these silver certificates put out under the Sherman
law were made payable in silver dollars, and as silver
declined, and these silver dollars declined in intrinsic
marketable value till they were worth little more than
fifty cents each, the silver certificates would have been
worth just the same but for the fact that it was the policy
of the government, regardless of the law, to keep all of
its money on a parity. It was its policy to make its promise, as was originally intended, fully good—to make all
of its dollars redeemable in 100 cents good money; therefore, the government accepted the silver certificates and
silver dollars as well, for all dues, made them interchange-

*See an article in this book, "Bank Note Circulation."

able with and practically redeemable in gold. Otherwise we should have had moneys of varying values. The silver and silver certificates would have been worth 55 or 60 cents, varying with the market value of silver, and other money actually based on gold would have been worth 100 cents.

So it may be seen that paper money cannot be issued against silver at a ratio of 16 to 1, and be full face value money, unless it be interchangeable with gold. And, as elsewhere clearly shown, the gold reserve is not strong enough to carry any increased volume of money.

Moreover, the government has directly lost an incredible sum making such experiments. Since 1873 it has bought for monetary purposes silver costing five hundred and nine million dollars. (See report, 1894, Bureau of the Mint.) The shrinkage in value from the average cost of $1 per fine ounce has been enormous.

These experiments were forced on the government as "compromises" by advocates of free silver coinage.

The New York Times, in a series of carefully prepared articles, based on actual statistics, lately showed that the losses to the government on fiat paper money and silver, have cost it more than two thousand millions of dollars. And the policy that prompted such money has cost the country more than five thousand millions of dollars. This estimate is far within the true loss.

The financial policy of the United States, dictated for twenty years by the mining camps of the West, would have beggared and bankrupted both the government and the people, if the country had not been new, and the most resourceful on earth.

Theorizing is well enough for dreamers, but in matters of business, common sense and well known principles are the only safe guides.

Free silver politicians who want votes, and Western mine owners who want other peoples' money at any cost, to the other people, have a theory never tried under like conditions in any country in the world, and they would commit us to that theory in complete disregard of conse- quences.

"DISCRIMINATION" AGAINST SILVER.

I have before me the U. S. Treasurer's report for 1894, in which it is estimated that in June, 1878, there was in the country a total silver circulation of only $87,693,789.

The free silver advocate claims that since 1873 there has been unrighteous and criminal "discrimination" against silver. But what are the facts? Up to 1878, the entire coinage of the country for a century had given us a total accumulation of only about eighty-seven millions of dollars; but since 1878 the coinage has been so great that we have now an accumulation of six hundred and twenty-five millions of dollars.

In other words, seventeen years ago we had about one-seventh as much silver money as we have today. Our stock has increased five hundred and thirty-eight millions in seventeen years. And by far the largest annual increase was in the years 1890-1893, when prices were fast declining.

Does this look like discrimination? Not only has there been this incredible increase, but the entire stock of silver dollars is made a full legal tender; and notwithstanding the fact that the intrinsic and marketable value of this mass of money has been for some time at a discount of nearly 50 per cent. from its face value, and its legal tender, or debt-paying value, it is made as good as any other money for all practical purposes. This parity has been maintained at a cost to the country of tens of millions of dollars of gold, and also to the great disturbance of all business and commercial relations.

The truth is, that all financial legislation for twenty years has tended directly to the vastly enlarged use of silver as money, increasing its use as shown seven times in seventeen years. The effort has failed in so far as concerns its actual circulation as money, owing to the fact that people will handle but small quantities of it. They turn it into the banks, and the banks turn it into the treasury and get other money in exchange for it; and there it lies idle and useless, serving only to disturb confidence in our financial system. As stated elsewhere, there are now only fifty-six million silver dollars actually in circulation, this being all the country appears willing to use. Then why should we want to coin any more silver? Why should we want free coinage or limited coinage?

Inasmuch as little more than one legal tender dollar in ten of the present stock of silver can actually be put into the channels of business, would it not be better to quit agitating its further coinage, and quit disturbing confidence in the basis of our financial system?

It is pertinent in this connection to suggest, that if the increased or decreased use of silver as money has anything to do with "prices," as the free coinage advocate claims, prices ought to have been going up at a rapid rate during the past seventeen years.

The ingenious author of "Coin" has figured to a nicety that the decline in wheat has been almost exactly the same as the decline in silver.

From the same point of view, "prices" ought to react with the increased use of silver; and if wheat was worth, say (for easy illustration), $1 per bushel in 1878, it ought now to be worth $7 per bushel, since we now have seven times as much silver money as then. Coffee was worth 11 cents per pound in 1878, and ought therefore now bring 77 cents.

All such figuring and reasoning are the foolish straining of a foolish theory, and have no basis whatever in fact. And yet upon this idea rests almost the entire claim for unlimited coinage of silver.

" DEMONETIZATION " OF SILVER.

"Demonetization" is a word used in this connection with much looseness, and is generally misunderstood. It is a favorite word with writers and speakers careless of what they say, or who intentionally deceive and misrepresent the facts. And many persons are led to believe that "demonetization" means an attempt to abandon the use of silver for monetary purposes.

All silver dollars now in circulation are a legal tender for the payment of all debts, public and private, and the government makes no discrimination whatever against silver money. All legislation has been directly in favor of the metal in the attempt to support it, and in conse- .

quence, the "discrimination" has really and seriously been against gold.

(The old Trade Dollar is not a legal tender, and for that reason went out of use. It is not supported by the government gold reserve, and consequently it cannot be exchanged for a gold dollar nor for a legal tender silver or paper dollar. It is, therefore, worth only about 50 cents, although it has the dollar stamp of the United States on its face. This is clear proof of what our silver money would be worth if it were not interchangeable with gold. The mere stamp of the United States, or of any other country, could not make it worth, in purchasing power, more than about 50 cents, its commercial value in weight.)

The repeal of the Sherman law did not in any way affect the $625,000,000 of silver now in the treasury, and in circulation, unless, indeed, it strengthened its value and its position as good money. The "gold bugs" are not trying to destroy the use of silver. On the contrary, all advocates of sound money want to continue it in safe quantities in use as good money.

The government has merely quit making any more silver dollars. That is all the "demonetizing" that has been done. The silver we have is as good, as money, as it ever was, and will remain so, unless the free coinage people succeed in putting us on a free silver basis, in which event it would not be worth more than half its present value, if, indeed, it would eventually be worth that.

And it would, for a time at least, be a good deal harder to get one of the cheap silver dollars under free coinage than it is to get a good silver dollar now, because all gold would go out of circulation, and we should have much less money than now, to say nothing of its greatly reduced purchasing power.

There is absolutely no "demonetizing" of silver in the sense the word is understood by the mass of voters. It is used merely to deceive and mislead.

THE " APPRECIATION " OF GOLD.

The free coinage people assert that gold has "appreciated" in value, and that its appreciation has depressed all other values. This, like very many other loose assertions from this source, has no foundation in fact. On the contrary, gold is vastly more abundant, and more readily obtainable, than ever before in the world's history. Its production and circulation have increased within thirty-five years more than twenty times the ratio of the increase in the world's population. This estimate is based on actual statistics of production.

About one-half the world's production of gold during the past 400 years has been produced within the last thirty-five years.* This fact, and the well known increase of gold as money within the memory of comparatively young men, completely refute the claim that gold is and has been "appreciating." Things or commodities do not "appreciate" when they become more plentiful.

Cotton has depreciated greatly in value because the crop has from year to year largely increased. Planters have attempted to secure a general agreement to reduce the acreage, believing that by so doing, and thus materially reducing the supply, they could "appreciate" its value and advance its price. The same general law must apply to gold.

It would be hard to demonstrate just what relation the volume of stable money has on prices, since they often decline or advance without apparent reference to monetary conditions. Supply and demand are more important factors than the volume of money. But common sense teaches that no particular kind of money can "appreciate" in value when the supply is largely increased, as in the case of gold. Through its large production only, silver has depreciated. And men now living may possibly see a depreciation in gold from the same causes.

With the present annual gold production, and the outlook for increased production, it is safe to say that the output for the next twenty years will equal the total product for five hundred years preceding 1860.

The output in 1894 was about one hundred and seventy-five million dollars; in 1895 it promises to reach two hundred millions. That is to say, the world will produce as much gold in 1895 as was produced in fifty years about the time America was discovered; or to come to more recent years, double as much as was produced in ten years from 1821 to 1830; nearly as much as was produced in the ten years 1831 to 1840; one-half as much as was pro-

*See table of world's production in report of Director of the Mint.

duced in the ten years, 1841 to 1850; more than a third
as much as was produced in five years from 1871 to 1875;
nearly half as much as was produced in five years from
1881 to 1885; and double as much, lacking a few millions,
as was produced in 1887. Since 1887 the production has
been more remarkable than during any other period of
the world's history.

Recent gold discoveries in Africa, South America, Australia and other parts of the world, are many of them rich
beyond computation. We are in a gold era, such as our
fathers, nor even we, ever dreamed of.

Inasmuch as more than one-half the gold production
for four hundred years has been within the memory of
comparatively young men, and inasmuch as that production is in a fair way to double before they become very
old men, the talk about the "appreciation" of gold is very
foolish; so foolish, indeed, that it will not be indulged by
well informed persons, unless for purposes of deception.
There is the greatest abundance of gold in all channels
of business in the great nations of Europe, and more than
one-third of the money of the United States is gold,
enough for all practical purposes if the free silver people
should cease to threaten to drive it out with cheaper
money.

GOLD THE "MONEY OF THE PEOPLE."

One of the theories of free coinage advocates is that
silver should hold its place with gold as money because
there is about the same amount in value of each in the
world. But they overlook the fact that it cannot be made
to circulate as money in considerable quantities. There
is, in the United States, $9 in silver per capita. But ex-
cepting the fractional silver used for change, there is only
about 80 cents per capita outside the treasury vaults, and
probably little more than half of that, say 50 cents per
capita, is in active circulation. The people find it too
heavy to carry about, so they use other money, and the
silver all drifts back to the government storage vaults.
The greater part of the gold of the country, however, has
always been in circulation. It is used largely in the settlement of bank balances, and it is a favorite money with

tens of thousands of the common people who put by small savings. A few gold pieces may be carried in the vest pocket, or put in a secret place without attracting attention or the danger of discovery; silver, more bulky and heavier, is less easily carried or concealed. Rarely is silver secreted if the holder has enough to exchange for a gold piece. Gold is really the "Money of the People," as is clearly evidenced by the fact that the people are now using about nine times as much gold as silver, silver change excepted, notwithstanding the fact that silver and gold exist in the country as money in about equal quantities.

In November last (see page 42, Report Bureau of the Mint) there was $500,381,380 gold coin in the hands of the people. On the same date there was only $56,443,670 in silver dollars in the hands of the people. On the same date (see page 41, Report of Director of Mint) the stocks of the two metals in the country were:

Gold...$626,632,068
Silver... 625,335,551

The following table shows the amount of silver dollars in actual circulation each year since 1885. (See Mint Report for 1894, page 23):

1886...$61,000,000
1887 62,000,000
1888.. 59,000,000
1889.. 60,000,000
1890.. 65,000,000
1891.. 62,000,000
1892.. 61,000,000
1893.. 58,000,000
1894.. 56,000,000

Round figures are given. This includes the silver dollars held by the banks, and handled by them at a loss.

These statistics are significant, and might be studied to advantage by "Coin," and others who preach free silver.

The simple figures show that gold and not silver is the people's favorite money metal.

On July 1st, 1894, the national banks which are popularly supposed to own all the gold in the country, held only $125,051,677 net gold coin (see report Bureau of the Mint, page 40), and only $34,023,000 gold certificates. That is to say, that out of $626,000,000 gold in the country, the national banks held about one-fifth.

It is a mistaken notion that there has ever been any "combination" among these banks to corner gold, and the simple figures make that fact plain without argument. The figures also show clearly that it is the people themselves who own and control the bulk of the country's supply of that metal. And it is largely held in small sums by the common people. Gold is indeed the money of the masses, and if the people are given the simple truth, and get to understand the facts elsewhere stated, that it is the single purpose of a large element of the free silver party to drive gold out of the country and leave only silver, they will turn a mighty cold shoulder to the deceptive pleas of the free silver advocates.

There is no doubt at all of the fixed and determined purpose of the Western mine owners, represented by their partners in Congress, to force the country to the single silver standard, with silver as the only coin in use. Any man who has carefully followed their course for ten years, in and out of Congress, sees and understands this as clear as day. They are playing a desperate game for what they believe to be large personal gains. They have been an absolute unit in aim, purpose and organization, standing shoulder to shoulder in every emergency, subverting all other public questions and interests to their own single common purpose of making the government the unlimited purchaser of the products of their mines. With an organization compact and intensely selfish and powerful, they have long practically held the balance of power in the Senate, kept the government wavering between sound and unsound financiering, wholly preventing a safe, consistent policy. They have for years pursued their end with restless and untiring vigilance and tenacity, hanging up important measures and blocking the public business at every step. Their complete organization and defiant attitude has time and again cowed and demoralized both houses of Congress. They have misled many good, able and honest law-makers and very many good citizens. They have influenced in their favor whole sections of country that would be impoverished if they should succeed in driving out the real "money of the people" and giving the people for money only such metal as they themselves have to sell.

The people have no time to study finances, nor to set a watch upon these ingenious, scheming and greedy agitators to discover their motives and plans; but they should be given the facts, plainly stated.

Several Western millionaires are now reported to be negotiating for one or more New York newspapers with which to influence people to vote additional millions into the pockets of the mine owners. These men care nothing about the welfare of the people. They merely want to sell silver at high prices to the government.

THE GENERAL DECLINE IN PRICES.

There has been a steady and persistent decline in prices since 1865, and the alleged "demonetization" of silver in 1873 neither checked nor hastened that decline. We emerged in 1865 from the greatest war in modern times. War is a great destroyer as well as a great consumer. During the war period the demand had greatly exceeded the supply in all lines. The sources of production had also been cut off, or reduced, and prices had gone sky ward. Decline was inevitable and immediately set in. Any one in the mercantile business during the period from 1865 to 1878 will remember distinctly the difficulty of selling at a profit any stock that lay a few months on the shelves.

The tremendous march of modern progress began about this time to become a great factor in the reduction of prices. During the period since 1870 the forces of civilization have developed more power and progress than in five hundred years, or even a thousand years, before that time. The great alleged "crime" of "demonetization" in 1873 did not create a ripple in the resistless sweep of modern ideas, invention, enterprise and development. Railroads have belted the earth, reaching thousands of miles into wonderfully rich and formerly unexplored regions, enlarging and cheapening beyond computation the production of every cultivated thing that grows from the ground, and equalizing (with cheap transportation, which has grown cheaper every year) all supplies in all parts of the world. Ocean tonnage has also been largely increased and carrying rates largely reduced. Steam has supplanted the sail; the six months' voyage of thirty-five years ago is now measured by days or weeks. Where capital was formerly tied up for weeks in an ocean shipment, it is now released within a few days. Where sales and purchases were made through months of correspondence by letter, the telegraph and cable now do the work in a few hours. The cost of doing a given volume of business is reduced by 50 per cent. All of these things have contributed to the steady and swift reduction of prices.

It should be needless to direct attention to the marvelous improvement and development in mechanical appliances within twenty-five years—a development probably exceeding that of all time from the days of Adam. The cheapening of all manufactured products has been in direct ratio to the increase and perfection of these appliances. And, they have also greatly reduced the cost of growing and harvesting wheat, corn, cotton and other agricultural products.

The unlimited coinage of silver could no more have stayed the effect of these forces than a bunch of straw would turn Niagara. They have simply developed new and strange conditions, whether for the good of mankind or the reverse remains yet an unsolved problem. But it would seem that in the end great good must come from the cheapening of the cost of all the necessities, comforts and luxuries of living. Labor problems, and many vexing questions and issues not now quite clear, must be adjusted. But silver has no place whatever in these adjustments.

We have had a transformation since the "demonetization" of silver. We are living in a new age. And the free silver advocates have as yet been unable to comprehend or accept the conditions. They have eyes but do not see. They cling to the dead past, and live on a pleasing but foolish memory. Some of them are garrulous and miserable. Others are spiteful and venomous, because they foolishly believe that the great marching procession has "conspired" against them and against the idol they have so long cherished with singleness of heart and pathetic devotion. They are mischievous, because some of them have filled high places. Many people are impressed with the tenacity of their devotion; others are attracted by the noise they make. But they are as unsafe guides as an old man in his dotage with a host of imaginary wrongs.

OLD TIME PRICES.

Who has not heard his father or his grandfather talk about prices in the days when there were no railroads—when every neighborhood was a market unto itself, and the silver "dollar of the constitution" was good enough for anybody?

How the dear old fellows like to talk of the good old days when farm hands got $60 a year and a potato patch thrown in for good count; when corn sold at 20 cents a bushel, sheep at 50 cents a head, and fine beef cattle, sleek and fat, at $8 and $10 each, average, for the "bunch;" when a strapping young fellow, brimful of vim and high hope, thought himself in luck and the envy of his fellows if he got a place in the village store at $75 a year and "found" himself; when the smart, lusty "chap" went to serve at a trade at $20 a year, a few coarse clothes, and a cot in the garret "to boot." Not many years ago the writer was wont to smoke a cigar after supper with a fine old gentleman who never tired in the recital of incidents of those days of good will and good cheer. And how he loved to dwell on the time when he entered the biggest store in his part of the state at $100 a year, being rewarded for faithful service with an additional $50 when Christmas came. Ah, those were piping times of peace and plenty! There were no "gold bugs" then. There were no national banks, with hated privileges. Anybody who could start a printing press could go into banking and issue money. True, the money had to be pretty well sorted before the old fellows started on a journey, and they were never quite sure it would be good when their destination was reached, but such inconveniences were good-naturedly accepted. There were no "conspirators" then to vex Uncle Sam and other honest folks. There was no "contraction" of the currency. The few millions of gold and silver were so widely and sparsely scattered that the most wicked ingenuity could get but little of it together; and as to the paper, the "bankers" who put it out, it being their own product, were never in a hurry to get it back; and so great indeed was their reluctance to call it, that much of it is out to this good day.

The great "crime" of the age had not then been committed. Silver had not then been "demonetized." And I have sometimes thought what a happy circumstance it would have been if some of the "friends" of silver had lived at that time, when nobody had ever thought of "discriminating" against their cherished metal. But the prices then would have been harrowing to their souls, free coinage and silver at a premium considered. "Prices" are a great worry to the "friends" of silver, as, indeed, they are to all the rest of us. Even corn at 45 cents a bushel and labor at 90 cents a day, with "demonetized" silver, vexes them beyond measure; and it would not be safe to say what might have been the effect of Peffer, Stewart and Bland, for instance, if they had seen free silver, with farm wages $5 per month and corn 20 cents a bushel. But the writer trusts he may be pardoned the wish, which ought not be an unkind one, that these three, and a few others, had indeed been of that generation. Possibly some of them were living in those days; but if so, free and high price silver and corn at 20 cents must have cost them many serious and painful reflections, which, however, they have doubtless forgotten. Silver at 16 to 1 was more valuable than gold (there being mined then several thousand million dollars less than now), but there were no sky-scraping prices of farm products, which is a curious circumstance, from the Stewart-Peffer point of view.

SILVER AND WHEAT.

The world's production of wheat has grown from two thousand four hundred and thirty-three million bushels in 1891 to two thousand six hundred and forty-five million bushels in 1894. This is a gain in supply of two hundred and twelve million bushels. But a more significant fact, and one of greater concern to American agriculturalists, is that the wheat exporting countries of South America and Russia have in this period gained two hundred and fifty-six million bushels in wheat production. That is to say, in 1894 Russia and South America had two hundred and fifty-six million bushels more wheat to sell in competition with the wheat of the United States than they had in 1891. And a matter of still greater significance and concern is that the large export surplus of fifty million bushels of the Argentine Republic last year was produced at a cost estimated not to exceed thirty-four to thirty-seven cents per bushel laid down at the seaboard shipping point.* Considering these facts, and the enormous crop harvested in the United States in 1894, is it necessary for the American farmer to puzzle his brain for an explanation of the low price of wheat? Is silver somehow at the bottom of it, as is foolishly stated in "Coin's Financial School," or is it a tremendous overproduction and a completely glutted market? Is it the "crime" against the product of the Western silver mines, represented by Stewart, Peffer, and associates, or is it the result of the opening up and cultivation of vast new tracts of the Lord's bountiful earth?

There was more coined silver and more idle money of all kinds in the United States in 1894, when wheat touched its lowest price, than ever before. The New York Times, of March 25th, 1895, from which the statistics are taken, commenting on the effect of over-production on prices, says:

"The natural effect of such increase, in exporting countries, on prices, can easily be seen. It may be noted, also, that Russia has an export surplus of 192,000,000 bushels of rye, against 70,000,000 bushels a year ago."

This item of 122,000,000 bushels increased surplus of a cereal largely substituted for wheat in many countries has been an important factor in determining prices.

The depression of business and the blocking of all kinds of enterprise on account of silver agitation has also contributed something toward depressing wheat. People cannot buy bread freely unless they have work. Capital, too, has been timid of investment in wheat, as in everything else; and the withdrawal of this sustaining influence has been an important factor in the sagging of prices of all commodities.

---

*Estimates by the New York Times.

SILVER AND COFFEE.

Reversing the order of wheat and cotton, coffee has advanced gradually and enormously during the past ten years.

The writer, being at the time in the wholesale grocery business, remembers that about 1885 he bought coffee in New York at about 7 cents per pound for fair grades. It is now worth about 18 cents per pound.

Silver was worth $1.06 per ounce in 1885. It is worth a little over 60 cents per ounce now. If the price of silver regulates the prices of other things, why has coffee gone up nearly 300 per cent. in ten years and silver gone down nearly 50 per cent.?

The explanation is simple, and is the simple explanation that applies to the rise and fall of wheat, corn, cotton and all other products, whether of the mine, the mill or the farm.

The production and supply of coffee in 1885 was excessive. More coffee was produced than the world could well consume. High prices in former years had greatly stimulated its production, and an undue number of people went into coffee growing. The increasing supply overstocked the markets, and prices gradually declined.

And when they got so low that coffee production became unprofitable, the industry was abandoned by many producers. The supply was gradually reduced, and stimulated by short crops, coffee went up. Another period of low prices in coffee, brought about from the same causes, is likely after a time to set in.

The decline or the advance in the price of silver has no more influence on the marketable value or prices of things than the remotest star in heaven on the tides of the ocean.

SILVER, WHEAT AND COFFEE.

Brazil produces a large per cent. of the coffee grown. The Argentine Republic produces a large amount of wheat.

Now in Brazil coffee has advanced in ten years from say 6 cents per pound to say 16 or 17 cents per pound on the Brazilian seaboard.

But note the contrary course of wheat in the Argentine Republic. In 1885 the cost of wheat in that country exceeded $1.50 per bushel. It is now about 40 cents. The greater part of the crop of 1894 was sold by Argentine farmers at about 38 cents.*

In other words, the wheat product of Argentina, and of the world, gradually grew till it exceeded the demand, while, on the contrary, the supply of coffee in Brazil and other coffee countries grew less till the demand exceeded the supply.

Silver had nothing whatever to do with the rise or the fall of either.

SILVER AND COTTON.

For the five years, 1890-1894, inclusive, the total production of cotton in the United States was, in round figures, 44,000,000 bales. For the previous five years, it was a little above 34,000,000 bales. That is to say, in the years 1890 to 1894 we grew nearly 10,000,000 bales more cotton than in the preceding five-year period. The production also increased in other countries.

With such tremendous gain in supply, with an actual and substantial falling off in consumption during part of this period (the falling off amounting to about 500,000 bales in 1893), need we look up the market price of silver to account for the price of cotton?

If the world grows more cotton than it can sell to the spinners and other manufacturers, what is to be done with the surplus? People cannot eat it, build houses with it, or otherwise use it. Somebody must hold it; put money into it; pay interest, storage and insurance; give it time and attention. The contingencies of future consumption and supply must be taken account of. The surplus becomes purely speculative, at greatly reduced value. And it brings down the price of the entire supply. With a large surplus on hand, and a production of ten million bales per year in the United States (an excess of

---

*Estimates made on gold values.

two million bales per annum above legitimate demands from this country), with no certainty, or even reasonable probability, of decreased production, can anybody fail to see why cotton is lower than ever before? The state of Texas alone grew last year nearly half as much cotton as was grown in the entire South ten years ago; and the production in that state can be largely increased at a profit, even at present prices.

If silver were 30 cents, 75 cents, $1.00 or $2 per ounce, would the present large surplus of cotton and the overproduction in the United States of two million bales per annum disappear? It would if the decline in silver has been the cause of the decline in cotton, as the fertile author of "Coin," and other visionaries have figured; but a practical man would say that the crops must be reduced two million bales, or new uses must be found to consume two million bales more than the world now consumes, if the old standard of prices are again to prevail.

SILVER IN FRANCE.

Free coinage orators point to France as a country that has done wonders with silver. But when silver began to decline, and its coinage ratio to go below the gold value, France closed her mints to silver.

A recent statement of the Bank of France* showed specie holdings as follows:

Gold..$430,000,000
Silver.. 225,000,000

Showing $205,000,000 more gold than silver.

The November statement of the United States Treasury showed specie holdings:

Silver..$508,000,000
Gold... 126,000,000

Showing $382,000,000 more silver than gold.

So it appears that the Bank of France held nearly $2 in gold to every dollar in silver, while the United States Treasury held only $1 in gold to every $4 in silver.

The Bank of France, on the date referred to, held nearly double as much gold as the Bank of England; and France is as firmly a gold standard country as England, and will

*See 1894 Report of the Director of the Mint.

always remain so. And it was wise enough to stop the
coinage of silver before it endangered its gold supply.
There is no free coinage party in France, nor, indeed, in
any other great civilized country, excepting the United
States.

France has a total of $825,000,000 of gold and $492,000,-
000 of silver, nearly double as much gold as silver, while
the United States has almost equal quantities of each.

FREE COINAGE IN MEXICO.

Our next door neighbor, Mexico, has produced more
silver than any country in the world. The mines of Chi-
huahua alone have produced more than five hundred
million dollars. Sonora, Zacetecas and others have
yielded even more. Coinage is free in Mexico. And yet
the people are poor beyond the conception of the common
American laborer. All labor is poorly paid. The writer
spent some time in Mexico some years ago, and made particular inquiry as to wages paid in agriculture and mining, the principal industries of the country, and found
them varying from 10 to 36 cents per day, which is equiv-
alent to 5 to 18 cents in American money.

The average for the farm laborer did not exceed 20
cents per day, or about 10 cents in our money. The people live in huts, subsist on the coarsest food, and $2 in
American money would buy the average outfit, from head
to foot, in clothing.

This is the condition in a free coinage country that has
produced more than four thousand million dollars of silver, and which is still producing silver at a larger ratio
per capita than any other country in the world, its exports
of the metal in 1893 being $51,000,000, and in 1892, $49,-
000,000. I have not the statistics for 1894. Mexico has a
population of 12,000,000. If the United States produced
silver in the same proportion or the same rate per capita,
counting Mexico's exports only, our production would be
$300,000,000 annually, yet who would say that the people
of that country are better off than we?

Mexico has a money circulation of $4.71 per capita.

A low rate per capita exists in nearly, if not quite all,
silver countries.

The people who advocate free coinage in the United States claim that low prices and depressed trade conditions are due to our gold standard, and insist that free coinage would bring an era of prosperity. If any of them will move across the border into Mexico their opinions will undergo a decided change. A move merely to the border will have a wholesome effect.

On the Mexican side there is small progress and unfavorable conditions generally, while within the United States line there is activity, growth and fair prosperity. All the cities and villages near the line are built and are building on the American side.

Free silver coinage can make no country prosperous; on the contrary, the mere apprehension of it is quite sufficient to depress business and arrest enterprise in any enlightened, prosperous nation.

TRAIN LOADS OF SILVER.

"Coin," with a stick twenty-two feet long, deftly measures off a space which he says would hold all the gold in the world; which, it may be said, is the strongest argument he could have made in favor of gold as money.

He then neatly disposes of the world's silver money by saying that it could all be stored in a Chicago banking room and basement.

His idea is original, but he does not put it in a way that his pupils quite grasp the enormity of the pile. It would be a little more understandable if he had said that there is enough coined silver to load fairly well three hundred trains of twenty cars each, or a total of six thousand car loads. He might have explained further that there are eight hundred and forty-four car loads of silver held for monetary purposes in the United States; and also explained that it is impossible to keep more than seventy-six car loads of that outside of the Treasury, of which probably forty or forty-five car loads are stored in bank vaults; showing that thirty or forty car loads are as much as the people are willing to carry about in their pockets and secrete in their homes.

The United States produced in the single year 1893, one hundred and four car loads of silver, almost three

times as much as the people will carry about with them,
and more than twice as much, excepting silver change,
as can be kept in circulation outside the Treasury.

In 1893 the world produced two hundred and eighty-two
car loads of silver. The production had since 1874 increased in every year, excepting one; and would have continued to increase more rapidly but for the fact that it began to decline in price because it became so abundant it
could not be utilized either as money, or in the arts.

Owing to the improved methods of mining within very
recent years, and discoveries of new mines and mining
regions in different parts of the world, it is perfectly safe
to say that if silver had remained at even the greatly depreciated price of $1.00 per ounce, not less than $300,000,-
000 or say four hundred and five car loads, would have
been mined in the year 1895—about ten times as much
as the people of the United States keep in active use.

At this rate of production 22,500 car loads would be
turned out in an ordinary lifetime. All the locomotives
on the largest system of railroads in the world could hard-
ly haul it.

And the capacity of production is unlimited. If its
value could be raised even to 84 cents an ounce, its price
in 1893, its output would now far exceed the two hundred
and eighty-two car loads mined in that year. But in the
face of unlimited quantities in sight, and unlimited resources for getting it out of the mines, no great or permanent rise in its price is possible. And under such conditions its constant fluctuation in value is inevitable. If
the price is so low that little is mined, it will go up; if it
advances enough to show a profit enterprise and capital
will at once increase the output, and it will go down. The
output is limited by the price only.

The principle is the same as in pork production. If
hogs are high, farmers everywhere go to raising them;
and soon glut the market. Then the price of pork de-
clines till hog raising becomes unprofitable; and the
farmer tries his hand at something else.

Does anybody want a currency based on such a metal,
a currency that a lot of miners put up or down as their
interests prompt? Today you have Dollars, tomorrow
you have—What?

GOLD AND SILVER PRODUCTION.

The world's total stock of metallic money is approximately $8,600,000,000, the proportion of gold and silver being not far from equal, there being about one-tenth more of the latter; say $4,100,000,000 gold and $4,500,000,000 silver.

This is the total money accumulation of these metals from the date of their use to the present time.

And it is interesting to note that the world's production of the money metals within the last thirty-five years has been approximately $7,300,000,000, of which about $3,950,000,000 was gold and $3,350,000,000 silver.

Much more gold than silver was consumed in the arts; and several hundred millions more silver than gold was, in that period, available for coinage into money.

This immense increased supply of the precious metals became the property of a few countries, since it was through the agencies of the progressive, civilized nations only that it was produced.

The gold was readily absorbed, owing to its great value in small compass; but these enterprising countries suddenly accumulated more silver than they could use as money. For instance, the silver of Mexico is mined largely by Americans and Englishmen, and its large output goes mainly to England and the United States. This is the simple reason why certain countries limited the coinage of silver. It is the reason why there can not be free coinage without involving these countries in hopeless bankruptcy.

In former periods the supply of the metal was limited, and the people had no more than they could handle and carry about, but the largely increased stock could not be circulated.

It is shown elsewhere that only about 80 cents of silver per capita can be actually circulated in the United States, and the same condition exists in all other countries where a lighter and more convenient currency is available.

Its "demonetization" by any country was not from choice, but from necessity. It was not done because any particular class of men or legislative body wanted it done, but because the people, in effect, said to the lawmakers:

"You are giving us too much of this kind of money; it is too bulky and heavy; ten or twenty dollars weights the pocket; we cannot hide it; when we have money we do not want everybody to know it; you can coin it if you want to, but if you do so you must keep it; if you give it to us we will give it back to you in exchange for more convenient money."

Any great change in the laws of any country has its source in the people. The people of certain nations of Europe decreed by their acts that the coinage of silver must stop.

The people of the United States have passed a similar decree. And in this decision, all the silver bugs as well as the gold bugs, have joined; the free silver advocate is no more willing than the sound money man to accept pocketfuls of silver in payment of accounts. If he gets $50 of the metal he strikes a bee line for a bank and converts it into paper or gold, or places it to his credit, and draws out paper or gold as he wants it. He has directly aided in its "demonetization," and in depressing its commercial value. Although he cries "free silver," he carries bills or gold in his pockets, and leaves the silver for the government to hoard in idleness.

And the United States Treasury's hoard of silver is absolutely idle and useless. The 1894 report of the Bureau of the Mint places the sum at $514,000,000. It is almost worthless as an asset, because there is no possible way to use it. Pensioners, contractors, and employes of the government, whether free silver advocates or otherwise, refuse to accept it in payment for services and bills.

For the same reason it is worth nothing as a support to the credit of the government. On the contrary, it is, for good reasons, a peril and a menace.

Any other government would melt much of it down and sell it; but the Western mine owners hold the balance of power at Washington, and they do not want it put on the market in competition with their product.

If gold could be obtained for a good part of it, the whole country would soon have great cause to rejoice. Such a deal would be a great bargain and a great blessing. Our fiat money would have substantial support, and our national finances could be handled with ease and confidence.

Furthermore, the stability it would give would soon

largely increase our supply of good money, and our rate per capita.

The facts here stated and the statistics given make plain the causes of the decline in the prices of silver, and of the largely increased ratio of value between gold and silver.

FLUCTUATIONS IN THE SILVER DOLLAR.

The following table shows, in the years named, the fluctuation in the intrinsic value of the silver dollar:

YEARS.	HIGHEST.	LOWEST.
1876	99 cents	79 cents
1878	93 cents	83 cents
1879	91 cents	82 cents
1886	79 cents	71 cents
1890	92 cents	74 cents
1892	74 cents	64 cents
1893	65 cents	50 cents

Only years are given in which the change was most striking. Fluctuations, however, have been marked each year since the large overproduction of silver began to glut the market.

If the country had been on a silver basis in the year 1876, for instance, a dollar of any kind of money would have been worth in July, 1876, 79 cents, and in December, 99 cents. In the following year it would have been worth about 90 cents, and down again in 1878 to 83 cents; up again in 1879 to 91 cents, and so on through each year down to the present time. In 1893 it dropped from 65 cents to about 50 cents, a change in value of 23 per cent. in a single year.

The capacity of production being now practically unlimited, its fluctuation will inevitably continue.

Great hardship and uncertainty would result if wages, salaries, the products of labor, contracts and credits were based on such money.

And the poor man, who earns his living by the sweat of his brow, would suffer most. While at times the dollar of 95 or 99 cents might keep him in comfort, his wife and little ones would be sorely pinched when the dollar dropped to 65 or to 50 cents. His wages would not go up and down with the dollar, but his food and clothing would do so.

And furthermore, the uncertainty of values would so disturb the business of his employer that work would be precarious. His employment and subsistence would fluctuate with the output of the silver mine. He would be constantly on the ragged edge, and at the mercy of adventurous mine operators and speculators.

The wage earner, above all other men, is vitally concerned in a fixed, unchanging standard of money. His living is too slender to admit of the risk of change and speculation. He can not afford to base it on the chance of any industry, especially not that of silver mining.

The silver dollar appears to be a mighty good dollar now, since it buys anything that can be bought with any other kind of a dollar; but this is simply because it is braced up by, and made interchangeable with, the gold dollar.

But if it stood alone, without a law or a policy that makes it exchangeable for 100 cents in gold, its purchasing value would be as uncertain as the wind and weather.

It cannot be that any man who understands this matter favors free coinage of silver, which means a silver basis and unsteady money.

On a silver money basis all market values in the United States would change with the rising and setting of the sun.

STANDARD OF GRAIN MEASURE.

A bushel is the standard measure of grain. Contracts of sale and purchase are made on this basis. And it is a stable measure, because it does not change.

But suppose it were a fluctuating measure, a little more today, a little less tomorrow—what confusion would result! When the farmer sold his wheat he would be obliged to do a complicated sum in mathematics to find out how much he got for it.

Yet there would be less confusion in a changing grain measure than in a changing money measure, because the effect of the latter would be more general.

And a silver standard would be such a money measure because silver is a commodity of uncertain market value.

With a silver basis, or measure of money, the farmer would be at as great loss to know what he got for his wheat, barley, corn, oats and rye as if the bushel basis or measure of grain changed every day.

Gold is now the unchanging measure of money just as the bushel is the unchanging measure of corn.

Can any practical man desire to change either?

RATIO BETWEEN GOLD AND SILVER.

"Coin" has a good deal to say about the commercial ratio of silver to gold. He goes back a century or two and shows that this ratio was fairly steady through the period he goes over. This is true, and there were a number of good reasons for it, the chief being that the production of gold and silver were happily in about the proportions needed.

But it suits his purpose not to go further back than 1687. Prior to 1680, covering the period from 1493, there had been a change of 50 per cent. in the ratio.

~ The "appreciation" of gold and the depreciation of silver through this period is a very interesting circumstance in connection with the silver doctrine.

And the cause of the decline in silver was the same as now, namely, a largely increased production, though it worked more slowly for two reasons. First, owing to the fact that in former times there was a scarcity of both gold and silver, and it was not difficult to absorb as money all that could be had of either; secondly, all movements were slow a few hundred years ago; what is now accomplished within two or three years then required a century. The increased production of silver was slow, and though the quantity was comparatively small, the per cent. compared with production in former periods was great.

The commercial ratio of silver to gold in the 15th century was a fraction over 10 to 1. In the 17th century it was a fraction over 15 to 1. This was in 1680.

"Coin," conveniently, begins his table in 1687, and completely ignores the most remarkable change that ever occurred between the metals, the most remarkable owing to the general scarcity of money of all kinds, and particularly of the precious metals. And the change is clearly directly traceable to the ratio of production between the metals.

On pages 174 and 175 of the report of the Bureau of the Mint, 1894, may be found a table showing the production of both in the 15th, 16th and 17th centuries. In the early part of the 15th century the per centage of silver produced was very small, being from 1493 to 1520 only $54,-703,000, while the production of gold in the same period was $107,931,000. The ratio at that time was not far from 10 to 1. But the output of silver soon began to largely increase, and after 1544 the production of gold began to fall off. The following table from page 175 of the report shows the relative production in value of the metals during the period referred to:

| | Per Cent. of Production. | |
Year, A. D.	Gold.	Silver.
1493–1520	66	33
1521–1544	55	44
1545–1560	30	69
1561–1580	26	73
1591–1600	22	78
1601–1620	24	75
1621–1640	25	74
1641–1660	27	72
1661–1680	30	69

In 1680 the ratio of values stood at something over 15 to 1.

The above table explains the cause of the decline in silver in that period, and no argument is needed.

Its production largely increased, and that of gold largely declined. There was no "demonetization," or "unfriendly" silver legislation in that day. It could have been affected only by the natural laws of supply and demand. Considering the conditions then prevailing the decline was even more remarkable than the decline of 50 per cent. in the value of silver since 1873. In the latter period its output became so great that, owing to its bulk and weight the currency systems of the world could not absorb it.

The table referred to extends down to the present time, and, if considered with reference to general conditions and influences at different periods, is an interesting study. It gives convincing proof that a double standard of money value has at all times been uncertain. No proof ought to be needed that such a standard, on any basis, is now impossible, owing to the fact that there is now a real surplus of silver; and anything of which there is a surplus is of unstable value and purely speculative, subject to sudden and violent fluctuations. No such thing can furnish a safe financial corner stone.

No country can prosper on a money basis bobbing up and down. There could be no certain profit in business, nor any steady or satisfactory remuneration for labor, with dollars worth 60 cents today, and 55 or 65 cents to-morrow.

A silver standard in America would make it necessary for a man each day to wait the silver quotations from the London market to ascertain how much money he had, how much his neighbor owed him, or how much he owed his neighbor. As to wages, or the cost of living a month or year in the future, he could form small estimate. No equitable scale of wages could be agreed on between employer and employe. The money would be liable to go down in purchasing value till the workman could not live on his pay; or it might go up till it would bankrupt the employer. There could be no confidence between the men who give work and those who work. Frequent adjustments would be a necessity. Strikes and grievances would multiply; uncertainty in pay and profit, and dissatisfaction would become general.

If a man insured his life for the benefit of his family, he could make no estimate on what they would really get at his death. The sum might be more than he counted, or it might be a great deal less.

If he sold his house, or his farm, for a given sum, the note he took in payment would be in the nature of a lottery ticket; the money might go up, and the final payment be more than he expected, or it might go down and be less than he expected. If he were in debt the rise might enable him to square accounts with ease; or the decline might embarrass or cripple him. He might draw a prize or a blank.

It is doubtless unfortunate for mankind that silver has become so abundant that it is unsteady in value, and consequently uncertain and unsafe as a basis of money. It is also unfortunate for the farmer that overproduction and competition have so greatly reduced the price of wheat; but these facts exist, and it is more sensible to look them squarely in the face, than to theorize, worry, and upset things generally, in a vain effort to change them.

It may be unfortunate that gold is now the only money metal that has a safely steady value on which present or future obligations can with equal safety be based, but such is the case; and it does no good to fret and rail about it. Natural and irresistible agencies, controlled by no class of men, brought about this condition; and, if the condition ever changes, natural, and not unnatural agencies must bring the change. It can not be done by legislative edicts at Washington.

EXPORTS OF SILVER.

The production of silver in this country continues to add to our money circulation an amount equal to the marketable value of all the metal mined, less the amount used in domestic arts. The surplus is exported, and either brings an equal amount of gold into the country or keeps an equal amount of gold from going out. In 1894 we exported and sold abroad $39,555,879 of domestic silver. This silver either added or saved to our currency an equal amount of money. If it had been coined into money and kept at home, we should have been obliged to send abroad an equal amount of gold, unless we had increased our indebtedness to foreign lenders. The United States does not destroy silver when it quits coining the metal. It is sold, and our circulation increased that much. The increase creates no apprehension and is substantial. It is gold, and each dollar has an intrinsic value of 100 cents. If the silver were coined into dollars they would add more to the volume of circulation, but would possess an intrinsic value no greater than the export value of the metal; and its coinage would drive out more gold than the gain in silver circulation.

OBSTACLES IN THE WAY OF FREE SILVER.

If the currency of the United States were not on a gold basis, and there were no gold in circulation, the free coinage of silver could be accomplished without sudden shock and disaster, because no large part of the money would be withdrawn from circulation, suddenly contracting the currency; and also because there would be no sudden and violent unsettling of credits and values, and sudden with-drawals of foreign capital.   Under a well arranged note system, based on silver, there would be a gradual increase in the volume of money, and possibly a general rise in values; though so long as the paper were within safe limits higher prices would result rather than from the cheapening of silver, the basis of the money, from in-creased over supply, than from the actual volume of cur-rency put out.   Under such circumstances the free silver advocates could obtain their desire—an immediate in-crease in the money supply.

There are good grounds, however, for the belief that the United States would, under any system on a silver basis, be under serious disadvantages as a progressive nation, and that owing to these disadvantages its enterprises would languish; but if we were not on a gold basis, it could by free coinage doubtless make money, such as it would be, abundant, without the danger of serious dis-turbance for the time being, its fluctuation in value not considered.   (This assumption, however, it may be said is theoretical.)

This is what the free silver people desire to accomplish. But they overlook the fact that $626,000,000 of our money is gold, and that this part of it would immediately dis-appear, and by sudden contraction, disastrously defeat their purpose.   They ignore our foreign indebtedness of probably about $2,000,000,000, a large part of which would have to be settled, and soon take all the available gold, and much silver besides.

These are some of the difficulties in the way of free coin-age.   It would seem that they are simple and clear enough for reasoning men to see them.   They are so ap-palling that if we should ignore them we should become a nation of bankrupts and the wonder of the world.

Free coinage of silver means a silver basis, with silver as the only metallic money, and a loss to the currency of $626,000,000 gold.

DO WE WANT BIMETALLISM?

There was in the United States on November 1st, as elsewhere stated, approximately $625,000,000 silver and $626,000,000 gold.

Shall we use both the silver and the gold, or shall we use only one, and get rid of $626,000,000 of the other money?

To use both is bimetallism; to use one is monometallism.   Are we bimetallists, or are we monometallists?

England is practically a monometallic country, since it uses but $112,000,000 of silver, all told, and that as a limited legal tender.   China, Japan, Mexico and most South American countries are also monometallic countries, since they use only silver.   France and Germany are bimetallic countries, both using gold and silver; the latter in larger quantities than England, and a large per cent. of it as full legal tender.

France, next to the United States, uses more legal tender silver than any other bimetallic country, the amount being $434,000,000.

Germany uses $215,000,000, all told, only $105,000,000 being legal tender.

The United States has $549,000,000 full legal tender silver, $626,000,000 legal tender gold, and $76,000,000 silver half dollars, quarters and dimes, which are limited legal tender.   Both kinds of money, under our present laws and policy, are good, and both (excepting the fractional coin) a full legal tender for the payment of debts to individuals and of dues to the government.

Are we satisfied to keep and use them both in safe quantities or are we partial and obstinate, and shall we determine to use but one and drive the other out of circulation and out of the country?

I believe these are needless questions.

It would be hard to see what the country could gain and easy to see what it would lose by such a course.   The masses of the people of the South and North—ninety-nine in every hundred—are straight out bimetallists.   The writer is a bimetallist.   He believes with the ninety-nine in every hundred Southern and Northern men, in the use of both gold and silver, and all other good money we can get; but he does not believe in using more silver than can be handled with convenience to the people, and safety to the Government. He believes also that the coinage of silver should be regulated by its absorption as a circulating medium—by the amount the people are willing to take and use, and keep in circulation—its idle accumulation in large sums in the treasury vaults being useless and dangerous at the present ratio. He does not however believe in schemes to force the increased and inconvenient use of silver by the withdrawal from circulation of small denominations of paper money.

Now, how are we to continue bimetallism? The silver dollar circulates in the same channels as the gold dollar, of equal purchasing and debt-paying value.

But the gold dollar has an intrinsic and marketable value nearly double the silver dollar. It can be melted down and sold at the rate of about $20 per ounce, or for one hundred cents, in any country in the world, but if the silver dollar be melted down it can be sold for only about sixty-two cents an ounce (the present market price), or something over fifty cents. Then why does the gold dollar circulate with the silver dollar? Why do not the people melt down their gold dollars and sell them, and keep the dollars with less marketable value for use in paying obligations and making purchases?

Is it because the United States has put its dollar stamp on the silver piece?

No. That stamp, of itself, does not add the fraction of a cent to the value of the silver piece.

It is because the affirmed policy of the United States makes its silver dollar interchangeable with its gold dollar; and because it undertakes to keep not less than $100,000,000 in gold on hand, so that it may have an abundance of the dollars of one hundred cents marketable value to maintain the interchangeable quality of its cheaper, fluctuating silver money, and its otherwise worthless paper money. Thus we have bimetallism as the word is generally understood.

But it ought not to be hard to see that this $100,000,000 gold reserve is already subject to considerable strain. It supports all the silver, either in the form of coined silver or paper silver certificates, and all other forms of paper, making a total of about eleven hundred million dollars directly dependent on that reserve for its full face value.

Now, if under our present financial system we coin any more silver we increase the strain on the gold reserve, which alone makes all our money good. It is comparatively a small sum, say one-eleventh of the money it supports and gives value to. It could not have been kept on hand a week at any time since it was established but for the confidence the world has in the promises and integrity of the Government. One-eleventh of the fiat money taken to the Treasury window would have taken it all out. But trusting the Government's integrity of purpose, and its ability to maintain that gold reserve, none of it was ever drawn upon, except for purely commercial purposes, till the Sherman law was passed in 1890 providing for increased coinage of silver at the rate of $54,000,000 per annum, thus increasing by that amount annually the strain on that gold reserve. Serious financial disturbances followed. The gold reserve declined rapidly. The danger became so great and so imminent that the Sherman law was repealed in 1893, though with great difficulty, owing chiefly to obstructive measures of Senators from the mining districts of the West, who wanted to put the country on a silver basis. Full confidence has not yet returned. It was retarded by the appearance of a strong and determined free coinage element in the Fifty-third Congress.

Now, with these simple facts before him, stated in a straightforward way, the writer is sure that any candid man (though he may have advocated free coinage) must admit that the United States cannot coin any considerable quantity more silver without wiping out that gold reserve.

Admitting this, we get back to the question: Do we want bimetallism? Do we want to use both gold and silver as now, and have about $24* per capita good, full value money, or are we willing to drive out the gold for the sake of coining the product of the Western mines, and have, for a time at least, only about $16 poor money per capita, worth really only about $8 full value per capita? We would increase the $8 per capita as the Western mines turned out silver and as other countries

---

*The 1894 government reports estimate about $25 per capita.

might sell us their accumulation of the unwieldy metal. But we should be so hopelessly bankrupted that those of us now living would not feel much concern as to the future supply of the uncertain and cumbersome money.

That supply would probably eventually be abundant, though depreciating and fluctuating, and therefore constantly unsettling values and trade. But in the meantime, with money on the basis of $8, present purchase value, per capita, what would become of the people and industries of the United States—a people accustomed to $24 per capita, and enjoying credits to the extent of probably $15,000,000,000 or $20,000,000,000* based directly on that $24 per capita and on that $100,000,000 gold reserve?

Is there a man in America whose imagination would not stagger under an attempt to conceive the consequences of such a calamity?

While Mexico and the Western silver mines rehabilitated our currency with a metal which the people now absolutely refuse to accept in any quantity, and of which only about fifty-six million full legal tender dollars can possibly be circulated (a great part of that lying idly in the bank vaults), what would become of the idle, penniless men, women and children of the United States, with creditors like wolves swarming about them?

Is there any man who can read the plain, truthful statements here made and not understand them? And if he understands them, is he a bimetallist, or is he for free coinage and silver monometallism?

Of what avail are such sophistries, catching cartoons, ingenious illustrations, questionings and deceptive reasonings as are contained in "Coin's Financial School" when set against the serious facts and simple, naked truths of the real situation? It is little less than criminal to deal in sophistries and artful deceptions when such momentous interests are at stake.

We want bimetallism, and not silver monometallism.

---

*Including individual indebtedness credits are estimated at $40,000,000,000.

FREE COINAGE NOT FREE DISTRIBUTION.

Suppose it be admitted that the free coinage of silver would be a blessing, and would at once increase the volume of money in the country as a whole—in what way would it increase the supply in individual pockets?

How would it even increase the supply in non-silver producing sections?

Free silver does not mean that the government would coin and send it about the country on pack horses and in wagons inviting every man to help himself. There will be no "forty acres and a mule" distribution, unless it be to the Western miners, at the end of this free silver fight, no matter how it may terminate.

The metal is produced in the mining sections of the West. The people who mine it would have the privilege of sending it to the government mints and getting it coined into money. When coined it would belong to them.

They would not scatter it around among their friends in Georgia, South Carolina and Illinois. They would take it back to Montana and Colorado.

If vast quantities of silver were mined the people out West might accumulate vast quantities of money. The "silver bugs" of that section might become as rich and obnoxious as the "gold bugs" of the East. Denver might become a great money center, but what advantage would that be to the people of Alabama or Michigan?

There is already idle money by the hundreds of millions in some sections of the country, but the people of other sections cannot get it because they buy about as much as they sell, and have no favorable balance of trade to bring it to them.

If the silver barons of the West were multiplied by the score, and if all the followers of the mining camps were to grow rich and great, it is not easy to see how the farmers of Mississippi or Ohio would be benefited any more than they are now benefited by the vast accumulations of money stored in the vaults of Eastern banks.

If every tenth man in Colorado were made a millionaire, and the fortunes of all were in cash, that accumulation of money could no more put up prices than does the present hoards in the East.

The truth is that the supply of money has little to do with prices, which are based on the cost of production, but regulated by supply and demand. They are affected also by the state of credits.

Prosperity, which stimulates prices, depends upon safe credits more than upon the volume of money.

Money may be abundant, and prosperity wholly lacking; but credit cannot be abundant without prosperity.

Confidence, which is the basis of credit, increases the use and active supply of money. It is also a great distributor of money, a great equalizer of its circulation.

The advocates of inflation, whether by free coinage of silver, or other methods, destroy confidence and thus destroy the only rational means of securing what they really want, an active increase of the volume of money in the channels of trade.

They get hold of the wrong horn of the dilemma. They propose an artificial and consequently unsafe increase in the money supply, believing that they can thus increase the circulation and put up prices.

The plan inevitably works the wrong way. Too many distrust the scheme.

The money is locked up, nobody wants to invest, or to buy beyond actual needs, and prices go down instead of up.

Then the stump orator comes upon the scene, abuses the "gold bugs," and lays the consequences of this folly at the door of the "money power."

Free silver would reduce by half the value of all pensions, wages, life insurance payments, bank deposits, and other evidences of credit.

GOLD STANDARD AND PROSPERITY.

Free silver orators and writers claim that we have tried the gold standard since 1878, and that things have gradually grown worse, and that it is now time to try something else, meaning free silver. This statement is untrue

in every particular. The period from 1878 to 1890 was
in all respects the most prosperous in the history of the
country. The increase in population, the industrial
growth, the influx of foreign capital and the expansion
of enterprise was not merely extraordinary, it was marvelous. It was a development never equaled, or even ap-
proached, in any country in the history of the world. In
1878 the West was practically unsettled and undeveloped. Since then its broad acres have been brought under cultivation, and its hamlets have become populous
and prosperous cities. In 1878 the South practically had
neither capital nor manufacturing industries. Its iron
and coal were almost untouched; its railroads were lacking in traffic, in bad repair, without substantial equip-
ment or organization, and for eighteen years there had
been little new construction. In those twelve years three
and a half times as many cotton mills were built in the
South as were built during the previous one hundred
years. The increase of spindles was more than 350 per
cent. More capital was invested in mining and iron production, ten times over, than in the previous history of
the country since its settlement. The same activity and
energy prevailed in all lines of industry. The development of the West and Northwest was not less wonderful.
Denver, Kansas City, St. Paul, Minneapolis, Detroit and
Milwaukee grew from townships to big cities; the population of Chicago grew from a few hundred thousand to
a million of inhabitants. The North also enjoyed un-
equaled prosperity. In that period our stock of gold increased from $213,000,000 to $690,000,000, a net increase
of $477,000,000; our stock of silver increased from $87,-
000,000 to $440,000,000, a net increase of $353,000,000.
Deposits in State and National banks increased from
$800,000,000 to $2,200,000,000, showing in twelve years
the unprecedented increase of nearly 300 per cent. in the
savings and accumulations of the people. And in the
same period the bonded debt of the United States, about
which the free silver men make so much noise, was reduced from nearly $1,800,000,000 to about $600,000,000,
a great reduction of two-thirds or say, about $1,200,000,-
000 of the interest bearing debt of the country. The
credit of the nation was so improved that the rate of interest on government bonds was reduced from a five per
cent. to a three per cent. basis. Throughout the country,

as a whole, prosperity reigned, and if the people were not satisfied with the condition it was because contentment is not the lot of humanity.

It is certain that the Western silver barons were disgruntled through all these years, the brightest in the annals of any people, and they were persistently and surely undermining the confidence which made such magnificent growth and prosperity possible. Their movements were watched with keen and anxious interest the world over by the men of capital and enterprise, who had set the busy wheels of progress in motion. In 1890 they forced the passage of the Sherman law, the baneful effect of which almost criminal blunder is fully explained in other articles in this work, and is known to the whole world. Prosperity and progress were soon at an end. The country was no longer safely on a gold basis. Distrust, uncertainty and stagnation supplanted hope, confidence and activity.

The free silver people claim that if the Sherman law was the cause of these misfortunes that its repeal in 1893 ought to have removed them. Such argument is extremely foolish. It is a fact well known to the world that the Fifty-third Congress was practically a free silver body. The failure of a bill to sustain the faith and credit of the government was greeted with cheers from members in the lower house. It is also loudly and vociferously heralded by free silver advocates that the doctrine is spreading and taking deeper root in all parts of the land. With our gold standard so vigorously assailed since the day the Sherman law was repeapled, and its very existence in such grave doubt, no well informed, well balanced man would argue that the country is, or has been since 1893, in position to further test the merits of the gold standard. But as any candid man must admit, its merits were fully tested from 1878 to 1890, and with results that amazed mankind. But in 1890, as stated, its existence was threatened, and that folly also amazed mankind, excepting only the advocates of free silver.

THE LOSSES OF 1893.

It has been claimed that the banks "combined" to raid the Treasury and bring on the panic of 1893. It ought not be necessary to combat this absurd contention, but so many people believe it to be true that it may not be amiss to show who sustained the losses of that calamity.

The New York Herald estimated, from actual market quotations, that within a short time the shrinkage in the value of stocks and bonds listed on the New York Stock Exchange was $700,000,000. These stocks were largely owned or held by banks as collateral for loans. Scores of operators in Wall street were beggared. Nearly 700 banks throughout the country, many of which afterward became wholly insolvent from sudden shrinkage of assets, were forced to close doors. Capitalists and investors suffered in proportion. The total losses directly and indirectly sustained by the monied interests of the country amounted to thousands of millions. Banks that did not fail, lost heavily, suffering in many instances serious impairment of capital. Deposits shrunk from 25 to 75 per cent., and banking for a time, to say nothing of losses, was wholly without profit; and owing to general stagnation and uncertainty, there has since been no money in the business.

Even the free silver advocate does not claim that the bankers and capitalists of the country are fools. Yet this is the only conclusion if they really "combined" to bring on that panic. Such losses surely follow all panics, and nobody understands this so well as the man who handles money.

To stay the general disaster at the time, the New York banks imperiled their own safety by loaning money to banks in every part of the Union. I doubt whether there would have been a dozen banks with open doors in Tennessee if aid from the New York "gold bugs" had been refused, and the ruin of business men and borrowers of all classes would have been complete. What is said of Tennessee was true in greater or less degree of all Southern and Western states. The "gold bugs" used clearing house certificates at home, and at great risk sent good money throughout the land in answer to the general cry of distress. These facts are well known to every well posted man. The writer believes that these bankers have made some mistakes in policy, as all men do; but whatever their errors of judgment, they have never "conspired" against the government or people, and the free silver sections of the South and West owe them a debt of gratitude that must remain long unsettled.

It may be added that the reason bank men, almost as a unit, oppose free silver, is not that they want to "conspire" against anybody, but because they so thoroughly understand the disaster that would follow. They know that its increased coinage under the Sherman act brought the panic of 1893. They do not guess or think that this was the cause, but they know that it was. And they do not want any more silver panics, particularly not a free silver panic, which they also know would be the worst of all. They know that they could not stand the consequent losses, and they know that the people could not stand them. The only selfish motive they have in trying to maintain the present gold standard is to restore prosperity to the country, and consequently to restore their former earnings and profits. This is a kind of selfishness common to all men.

This article is not intended in any sense as a vindication of bankers and monied men, but merely to remove mistaken notions which are in the way of sound money legislation.

Men send for a doctor when they are sick, a lawyer when they want legal redress, a preacher when they want spiritual comfort, a plumber when the water pipe bursts; they go to an architect when they want to build a house, send the horse to the blacksmith when they want him shod, engage a gardener to turn the ground and plant seed, and hire a rail splitter when the farm needs fencing; but when finances get out of joint, they abuse and turn a deaf ear to the men who handle the money and know most about it. There is a flaw somewhere in this general way of doing things. It might be well for awhile as an experiment to have the lawyers shoe the horses and the rail splitters dose the sick. If the shoes pinched and the patients languished, these things would be in keeping with the clumsy tinkering and patching by novices of the nation's finances.

THE MONEY POWER.

Suppose, for the sake of argument, we admit the false notion that the "money power" is unreasonably prejudiced against silver. Is a remedy possible if applied only in the United States? And how can any legal remedy be applied? Money cannot be legislated out of bank vaults at home and abroad, and out of the pockets of the people, and put into circulation in the United States. We are not necessarily a borrowing people, and whether that policy be right or wrong we are not in condition, nor in position, to put a stop to borrowing. We must have foreign money, and also the use of home accumulations, to carry our obligations and to develop our resources. But can we pass laws to make Englishmen send over money to build our railroads; to make home capitalists build and operate furnaces, mills, open mines and buy our surplus lands, and to make lenders discount our notes and accept our bills?

When we agitate and approach free coinage all these people lock their money up. Home money lenders are alarmed and foreign capitalists look upon us with contempt. Industrial progress comes to a standstill. We may fuss and fume and beat the air all we are a mind to, but our impotent fury merely closes the money chests tighter. The people we rail at are not merely the Rothschilds, a few great financial concerns in England, and a few thousand bankers in America. That vague, greatly abused and little understood thing, the "money power," is a mightier force than even the populists claim that it is. It is the PEOPLE—the millions of intelligent, thrifty and prudent people who have put aside the accumulations of their industry. Every man who has saved and owns money, whether the sum be $100 or $100,000, or who holds the notes of his neighbor, who is a depositor in a savings bank, or who is an investor in securities, state bonds or mortgages, is one of the "money power." If his hoard be only $100 he is as easily frightened and runs to cover as quickly as the man with a million. He is, indeed, more apt to lock his money up and put it entirely out of sight and out of reach than the larger and broader holder. If you have anything to sell, you cannot sell it to him.

Price counts for nothing. If you ask him to join you in an enterprise, he laughs at you. If you would borrow of him, he shies at your collateral. He may not be learned in the science of money. He may tell you that he knows nothing about the financial question, but he knows how to make you pay if you owe him; and if you scare him, he knows how to lock up his money and keep it.

He may be a populist or a free silver advocate—many of these i have observed grip the purse strings tightest, and they generally grab for gold when they put money into holes or stockings—but whatever he be, he is one of that mighty army composing the "money power." There are some six or eight millions of them. They fill every vocation and avenue of life. They are lawyers, doctors, artisans, merchants, laborers, farmers, preachers, beggars, guardians, trustees, executors, capitalists, men and women, old and young. They own the stocks of the savings banks, the national banks, trust companies and other corporations; own the money deposits; and the officers of these institutions are merely the paid instruments used by them. If they heap money upon bank counters, these custodians of their earnings must use great care and discretion in the keeping and disposition of their funds. If they want the money they have committed to the care of the banks, whether to invest or to hoard, it must always be ready for them. The banker is branded with incompetency and disgrace, or with dereliction of duty and sent to prison, if he cannot pay. This is the "money power" that cornered money and brought on the money panic of 1893. Whatever may be the precipitating cause, it is the "power" that brings on all financial disturbances. It is the "power" which now distrusts the financial policy of the United States. It is the "power" which believes there is more silver in the mines of the world than can be safely used as money by the United States without driving out its better money—gold—and which fears great disaster from further silver legislation. It is a "power" which cannot be driven nor legislated into buying and selling, lending, building and developing. It will stand stock still till it gets ready to move. Raillery, threats and denunciation do not budge it. It is the power of human avarice and self-preservation. Show it gain, confidence, stability, and it welcomes you. Threaten it with free coinage of silver and depreciated money and it draws away in alarm, yet grim and resolute.

Since this almighty "money power" is afraid of free silver, and will again and indefinitely arrest every industry and enterprise in the country if that heresy be threatened or instituted, what folly and madness to fly in the face of it!

We want prosperity, and we cannot have it unless we fully satisfy the people who have money to invest, whether in small or large sums.

The free silver people do not look at the practical condition and situation of things. They have a theory, and reason in the abstract. They block progress and distress the country exploiting that theory. They would withdraw the corner stone of thousands of millions of credits and topple the whole financial and commercial structure experimenting with that theory. Practical men know that it is a mere theory, vicious and dangerous. It is a catching theory, because with it is coupled abuse of the "money power," which so many voters fail utterly to comprehend. The voter himself may be an important factor in the "money power," yet unable to understand it—be filled with prejudice and resentment against it. Any of us who are industrious and thrifty, and who have saved money, are part of that much abused and really potential "power."

Will a large per cent. of the voters of the country continue to blindly follow these free coinage theorists, or have they had enough of them and of the disasters that follow in their wake?

If we want to start our mills and give life to our enterprises, they furnish us no money with which to do these things. The worst and loudest of them merely want our votes and the fat offices we can give them. It is to the "money power" we must look for the means of paying our labor and handling our products. If we want to sell a farm, a horse, a crop of wheat, a bale of cotton, a town lot, we never think of the free coinage orator, but go to some person who belongs to the "money power" and strike him for a trade. Let us make friends with these people, and cast out utterly the theorists and designing demagogues, who would destroy us, professing (for our votes) to love us, and to be infinitely concerned for us.

"PRIVILEGES" OF NATIONAL BANKS.

National Banks have no "privileges," in the sense that they are a favored class of institutions. During, and for a time subsequent to the war period, when government bonds were low priced, and bore high rates of interest, there was a good profit in National bank note circulation, but that day has passed; and there is now a well defined loss to the National banks in the exercise of their "privileges." This has been the case for a good many years.

To issue $45,000 circulation now, a bank must invest $57,000 of its capital in United States bonds, to be deposited with the United States Treasury to secure its circulation. This estimate is based on four per cent. bonds at 1.14, about an average price for eighteen months.

The bank must then deposit $2,250 with the Treasurer to the credit of a fund known as the five per cent. redemption fund, leaving it the use of $42,750 on an investment of $57,000. Therefore it loses entirely the use of $14,250 of its capital. Money is worth eight per cent. throughout the South and West, and in other localities. Counting interest at eight per cent. the loss on this item annually is $1,140.

The four per cent. bonds mature in 1907—twelve years hence. At maturity the face value only will be paid. Therefore in twelve years the bank loses $7,000 premium it paid for the bonds. The annual loss on this item is $583.

There is a tax of one per cent. on the circulation. The loss on this account is annually $450.

These three items constitute the principal cost of the National banking "privileges."

There is but one item of profit, which is the interest on the bonds. This for twelve months is $2,000.

Therefore, at the end of the year, the account stands as follows:

Interest on the $14,250 item	$1,140
Annual loss on the $7,000 premium item	583
Tax on circulation	450
Total loss	$2,173
Less interest on $50,000 bonds	2,000
Net loss to bank	173

Counting the $14,250 item on a basis of six per cent., there would be an apparent profit of $112; but it would be apparent only. Other items of expense incident to the system would much more than wipe it out. But I base the estimate on eight per cent., as it is in the East only and in the money centers that lower rates prevail.

Other items of cost are National bank examiners' fees, $50 per year, if two examinations are made; the advertising of five annual statements; the exchange and express charges in keeping intact the $2,250 redemption fund, and in transportation of new issues of notes; loss in circulation while new notes are in process of substitution for old, or mutilated notes; attention and labor in making various reports, and other items of direct or indirect cost. It is safe to say that the "privilege" costs a National bank, issuing $45,000 currency, directly, not less than $350 per annum.

If the bank has a large line of deposits the cost is much more, owing to increased work in making examinations and reports.

In reserve cities banks are also required to carry twenty-five per cent. reserve, their own notes, and other specified moneys and sight exchange not counting as part of this reserve. The class of assets they carry and the kind of paper they discount is also prescribed by law or regulation.

A State bank, with equal capital and deposits, can make more money than a National bank. As at present constituted, the National banking system is a decaying system, and no new National banks would be organized but for the reason that the people trust them more than they do State banks, and the more readily patronize them. And this is an anomaly, considering the general prejudice against them.

It is readily seen that it is a mistaken prejudice. It is one that would soon disappear if the facts were known. As recently stated by the New York Journal of Commerce and Commercial Bulletin, this prejudice has much to do with the free silver sentiment of the South and other sections, and if pains were taken by the press to publish the simple facts, and make them generally understood, the most serious difficulty in the way of a simple and proper revision of our currency system would be removed.